Contents

Some words are in bold, **like this**. You can find out what they mean by looking in the glossary.

coyote

A coyote is a type of wild dog.

Coyotes are about as big as a medium-sized dog, such as a collie.

4

A Day in the Life: Grassland Animals

Coyote

Louise Spilsbury

Raintree

www.raintreepublishers.co.uk
Visit our website to find out more information about Raintree books.

To order:
☎ Phone 0845 6044371
🖹 Fax +44 (0) 1865 312263
🖳 Email myorders@raintreepublishers.co.uk

Customers from outside the UK please telephone +44 1865 312262

Raintree is an imprint of Capstone Global Library Limited, a company incorporated in England and Wales having its registered office at 7 Pilgrim Street, London, EC4V 6LB – Registered company number: 6695582

Text © Capstone Global Library Limited 2011
First published in hardback in 2011
Paperback edition first published in 2012
The moral rights of the proprietor have been asserted.

Edited by Dan Nunn, Rebecca Rissman, Catherine Veitch and Nancy Dickmann
Designed by Philippa Jenkins
Picture research by Mica Brancic
Originated by Capstone Global Library
Printed and bound in China by South China Printing Company Ltd

ISBN 978 1 406 21892 3 (hardback)
15 14 13 12 11
10 9 8 7 6 5 4 3 2 1

ISBN 978 1 406 21895 4 (paperback)
16 15 14 13 12
10 9 8 7 6 5 4 3 2 1

British Library Cataloguing in Publication Data
Spilsbury, Louise.
Coyote. -- (A day in the life. Grassland animals)
599.7'725-dc22
A full catalogue record for this book is available from the British Library.

Acknowledgements
We would like to thank the following for permission to reproduce photographs: Alamy pp. 16, 23 den (© Don Geyer), 19 (© First Light/Thomas Kitchin & Victoria Hurst); Ardea p. 17 (© Mary Clay); FLPA pp. 10, 12 (Minden Pictures/Michael Durham); iStockphoto pp. 6 (© Nathan Hobbs), 7, 23 muzzle (© Richard Rodvold), 9, 23 grassland (© Frank Leung), 14 (© Chad Zavala), 20, 23 cougar (© John Pitcher), 21 (© Andy Gehrig); Nature Picture Library pp. 11, 23 territory (© Thomas Lazar); Photolibrary pp. 13 (imagebroker.net/Bill Draker), 15, 23 howl (Alaskastock/Doug Lindstrand), 18 (Animals Animals/Joyce & Frank Burek), Photoshot p. 23 pack (NHPA); Shutterstock pp. 4 (© Denis Pepin), 5 (© Dushenina), 22 (© Wesley Aston).

Cover photograph of a coyote on top of a hill reproduced with permission of Shutterstock (© Denis Pepin). Back cover photographs of (left) a coyote's muzzle reproduced with permission of iStockphoto (© Richard Rodvold) and (right) a den reproduced with permission of Alamy (© Don Geyer).

We would like to thank Michael Bright for his invaluable help in the preparation of this book.

The author would like to dedicate this book to her nephew and niece, Ben and Amelie: "I wrote these books for animal lovers like you. I hope you enjoy them." Aunty Louise.

wolf

Coyotes are a lot like wolves.

But coyotes are smaller than wolves.

What do they look like?

Coyotes have grey fur on their backs and white bellies.

Their legs and feet are reddish-brown.

muzzle

A coyote turns its big, pointed ears to hear sounds from far away!

Its **muzzle** is reddish-brown.

Where they live

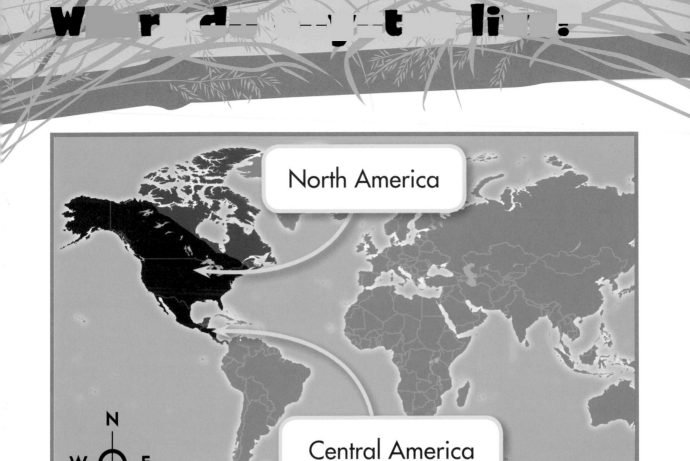

North America

Central America

N
W—⊕—E
S

key: ⬛ = where coyotes live

Coyotes live in North America and parts of Central America.

Many coyotes live in **grasslands**.

8

Grasslands are flat areas of land that are mostly covered in grasses.

In America, grasslands are often known as prairies.

Coyotes hunt for food at night.

They travel alone or in family groups called **packs**.

10

Coyotes live and hunt in an area called their **territory**.

They fight to keep other coyotes away from their territory.

W__t d___ __y __t __t.

rabbit

Coyotes mainly eat animals like mice, rabbits, and deer.

They also eat fish, frogs, snakes, fruit, and nuts.

Coyotes get most of the water they need from their food.

Sometimes they drink from rivers or ponds.

At night a coyote usually hunts on its own.

It uses smell and hearing to find small animals and then it pounces!

Sometimes coyotes hunt in **packs** to catch larger animals like deer.

They **howl** to tell other coyotes where they are in the dark.

What do coyotes do during the day?

den

Coyotes rest and sleep a lot during the day.

They sleep in a **den** that is somewhere safe and hidden from view.

Coyote dens can be holes in rocks or logs, or small caves.

Coyotes also sleep in dens that other animals, such as badgers, made and left behind!

W _ t _ r _ y _ t pups like?

Coyote pups have brown fur and big ears.

They drink milk from their mother and eat food that their parents chew up for them.

At first, the coyote pups stay in a **den**, day and night.

Later, they learn to hunt at night with their mother, until they can hunt alone.

cougar

Wolves and **cougars** hunt coyote pups.

Coyotes hide their pups in **dens** to keep them safe.

20

Wolves sometimes attack adult coyotes, too.

Wolves do this to stop the coyotes hunting the same animals they want to eat.

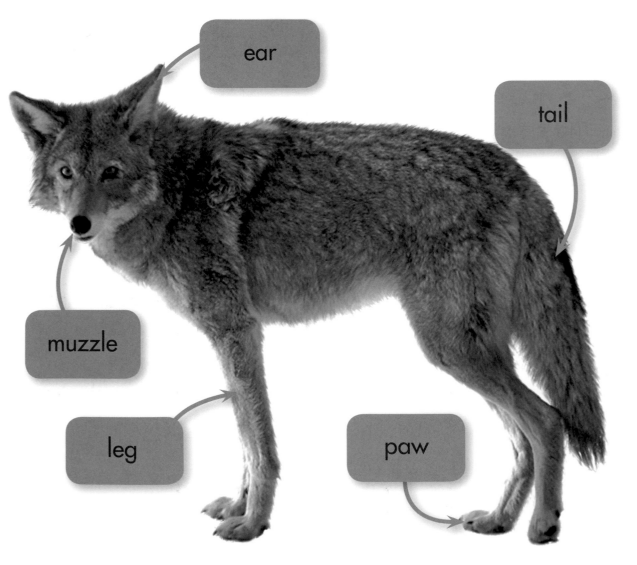

ear

tail

muzzle

leg

paw

22

Glossary

cougar large wild animal that lives in North America. It looks like a cat.

den hole in the ground or a rock where a wild animal lives

grassland land where mostly grasses grow

howl long, loud crying noise

muzzle nose and mouth part of an animal's face. A coyote or a dog has a muzzle.

pack group of certain animals. Coyotes live in packs.

territory area of land belonging to an animal or group of animals

Find out more

Books

Crafty Canines: Coyotes, Foxes, and Wolves, Phyllis J. Perry (Children's Press, 2000)

The Coyote (Nature Walk), James Bradley (Chelsea House Publishers, 2006)

Websites

http://animals.nationalgeographic.com/animals/mammals/coyote.html

http://www.nhptv.org/natureworks/coyote.htm

Index